How Puppies Grow

By MILLICENT E. SELSAM Photographs by **ESTHER BUBLEY**

FOUR WINDS PRESS   NEW YORK

The author wishes to thank Dr. John Paul Scott
of Bowling Green State University for reading
the manuscript of this book.

Second printing, 1973

Published by Four Winds Press
A Division of Scholastic Magazines, Inc., New York, N.Y.
Text copyright © 1971 by Millicent E. Selsam
Photographs copyright © 1971 by Esther Bubley
All rights reserved
Printed in the United States of America
Library of Congress Catalogue Card Number: 72-77803

How Puppies Grow

Here are six little puppies.
They were born only a day ago.

They are tiny.
Their eyes are closed.
They cannot open them to see.

Their ears are closed.
They cannot hear.

But they can taste.
And they can touch
and feel each other.

Already they have found
the nipples on their mother's body
where they can suck milk.

These tiny babies need their mother.

They could not live without her.

She nurses them.

She keeps them warm.

She keeps them safe from harm.

Sometimes a puppy crawls too far away.
The mother dog goes to it.
She picks it up carefully in her jaws
and carries it back.

At first the mother stays with the puppies all the time.

But after a few days

she leaves them alone for a while.

When she leaves, the puppies cry.

They crawl around.

They cannot see where they are going.

But they swing their heads from side to side

till they touch each other.

Each puppy tries to get its head
over another puppy.
They snuggle together all in a pile.
This helps to keep them warm.

They grow quiet.
They fall asleep.

The mother dog comes back to feed her puppies.

She licks them.

This wakes them up.

They start to crawl

and move their heads around

till they touch their mother.

Then she lies down

and lets them nurse.

The puppies spend the first week
of their lives
eating and sleeping.

When the puppies are two weeks old
they try to walk.
They fall down a lot.
But they keep trying.

Their eyes are beginning to open now.
They see things around them
but not very well.

Now the puppies are three weeks old.

They can walk without falling down.

They can see much better too.

And for the first time

they can hear sounds.

A loud noise makes them jump!

They have a few teeth
and can eat some solid food.
But they still need milk
from their mother.
They go to her if
she doesn't come to them.

The puppies play with their mother
as much as she will let them.

They lick her head.
They chew on her tail.
They gently bite her ear, her
mouth, and her back.

By the time they are four weeks old
they play with each other a great deal, too.

They lick and chew each other...

They bite each other's ears...

They run after each other.

Now the puppies are five weeks old.
They are running and chasing and tumbling
and playing with each other all the time.

This is the way they learn t

endly with other dogs.

The mother leaves them alone
a lot of the time.
When the puppies see her,
they run after her and try to nurse.

Sometimes the mother dog lets them nurse.
But often she chases them away.
She may growl and snap at them.
This is the way she makes them learn
to do without her milk.

In the next few weeks
they eat more and more solid food.
They are growing up.

The best time to get a puppy
is when it is between six and eight weeks old.

It has already learned to
eat solid food.
It has already learned to be friendly
with other dogs.

Now is the time it can learn
to play with you.

It can lick your hand or your face.

It can nibble on your finger.

It can run after you.

It can learn to be your friend.